This book should not be used
as a substitute for real life experience
and the exercise of good judgment.

Visit **www.yourblackfriend.com**
for more answers.

A MoreMindful Creation

WHY DO BLACK PEOPLE LOVE FRIED CHICKEN?

And Other Questions You've Wondered But Didn't Dare Ask

Nashieqa Washington, M.B.A.*

**Why Do Black People Love Fried Chicken?
And Other Questions You've Wondered
But Didn't Dare Ask**

Your **Black** Friend
P.O. Box 1532
Venice, CA 90294

ISBN: 0-9777921-0-2

Printed in the United States

10 9 8 7 6 5 4 3 2 1 0

Dedicated to those who have taught me through their questions

About the Author

Nashieqa Washington, M.B.A.* aka yourblackfriend. com aka Pamela Moore, author of *Why Do Black People Love Fried Chicken? And Other Questions You've Wondered But Didn't Dare Ask* is a Black American woman. Undeniably her pen name and the letters following it helped to lure you in. A "Black" name lends ethnic credibility and the M.B.A. denotes experience through education. However, in her case M.B.A.* simply stands for Member of Black America. Don't feel duped, she has a degree in a traditional field of study but it is largely unrelated to the subject matter of this book.

Throughout her life the author has had the privilege of interacting with many different ethnicities. She was raised a military brat, incredibly made it through her own tour of military service and lives in ethnically diverse Southern California. Her life is greatly enriched by purposely seeking to associate with people from all walks of life. She accepts that these relationships will inevitably include answering questions about Black people. Since she can't be everywhere, and it is impossible to address everything you've wondered in this book, be sure to visit **www.yourblackfriend.com** for more answers.

Contents

Contents

II. Speech – Axe me again and I'll tell you the same 33

V. Traditions/Professional Life – Same as it ever was... 61

Message to the Reader

It is important to note at the outset that *Why Do Black People Love Fried Chicken? And Other Questions You've Wondered But Didn't Dare Ask* answers questions about Black Americans (aka African-Americans). For the record, there can be major cultural differences between African-Americans and other people of color you refer to as "Black" (e.g. Africans, Afro-Latinos, West-Indians, etc.). If you are already confused, it is essential that you continue reading.

The term "White" is used generally throughout the book for ease. Sometimes it specifically refers to ethnic Caucasians and at other times refers to all non-Blacks. I know that it's terrible to lump people together. However, anyone educated in a Eurocentric society is similarly conditioned by Western images of Black folks and comes away with similar ideas. As a result, it is very likely that you engage in somewhat predictable behaviors and have questions like the ones addressed in this book. Since this is a great opportunity to get your questions answered, I highly recommend reading on.

Unquestionably, this book could have been written from a more scholarly standpoint, however, that is a perspective with which few identify. As a "non angry Black woman" I've been able to compile these questions because of the level of comfort people felt approaching me and asking them. And sometimes it was simply safer to question me because I was a largely unknown to the individual and would remain so after our limited interaction. The questioners have ranged from those who have little or no contact with Blacks to those in intimate relationships (some marital) with a Black person. I have received questions so regularly that I am convinced that the publication of answers provides a much needed service. So with the hope of improving relations and in order to spare other Black folks, within these pages you will find the answers to many of your questions.

Disclaimer: The primary purpose of this book is to provide information about Black folks (variously known to you as African-American, Negro, Colored, etc). Please read with the understanding that neither the Publisher nor Author is engaged in race baiting, rendering sociological, psychological, or any professional advice. The overall goal is to educate and entertain. The Publisher and Author shall not be liable or responsible to any person or entity with respect to any damage caused, or alleged to have been caused, directly or indirectly by the information contained in this book.

It cannot be overly emphasized that this book cannot and does not strive to answer all questions, but instead seeks to complement, amplify, and supplement other texts. It is not the final word on any matter nor should it be taken as such. If you require more information please visit **www.yourblackfriend.com**, do some research, or try the person-to-person approach.

Preface

This book stems from my ongoing feeling of acting as Ambassador to Black American(s). As strange as that may seem, I've introduced and eased relations between more Black and White people than I can recall. Think about this for a moment, Black folks (initially Africans) have lived in this country about as long as your ancestors. Nevertheless we are largely unknown to you in any meaningful way. Stay with me here. We are strangers in the sense that you think you know us (through casual interaction, music, and mass media) but your actions and questions regularly betray your professed knowledge. For example, if you really knew Black people, you wouldn't wonder why it's okay for us to call each other nigger and not okay for non-Blacks (see Question #21). At any rate, we're certainly not as familiar to you as one would expect given our close history.

You do the Black dances, talk Black and some of you even walk our walk – but ask yourself how well you know your "Black friends" or Black people in general? Or more importantly, what do you think you know (i.e. what assumptions are you operating on) that keeps your relationships from being as close as they could be? Are your relationships with Black work and school associates the same as with friends that look like you (this analysis should not include anyone subordinate or obligated to you in any way)? Have you had to sublimate your identity to cultivate or maintain your Black friendships?

Or perhaps you use these relationships to make a public statement or as a form of rebellion (guess who's coming to dinner?).

You might protest these characterizations, but it's interesting to note that your friendships with Blacks are typically relegated to a diminished position in your social hierarchy. It could be that you sincerely desire more intimate relationships, but fear (of looking foolish or reprisal) has kept you from having the conversations or asking the questions that might actually bring you closer. For example, why do "they" (Black folks) do the things they do? Well, here's your chance to comfortably get some answers, increase your overall level of understanding and hopefully create better relationships. But remember, this is only one Black person's view. In answering questions, this book is only one means to an end and not an end in itself.

I know many of you are thinking that if you've gotten this far in life, why should you care? Well, for a couple of reasons. First, an open honest dialogue about the impact of race in America is long overdue. Incredibly (and erroneously) discussions about racism are still largely framed as only between and amongst Black and White people. The long-standing assumption is that racism (if we agree that it exists) impacts only these two groups. And because it presupposes an adversarial stance, holding fast to the flawed Black/White model effectively sustains a deep wedge between the groups. Clearly that contributes to ongoing misunderstandings and a lack of empathy.

Secondly, and of equal importance, is the overall lack of concern or desire to understand one's fellow man at the root of many societal ills. A general attitude of indifference (on both sides) has brought us to our current sorry conditions. I believe that once you are armed with the knowledge of a person's motivations, you might choose to respond differently to their behaviors. And you may never learn the answers to the how comes unless you ask the questions. Unfortunately, most people are reluctant to even admit the existence of a problem let alone try to get to the root of it.

So where to begin? Due to the prevailing negative characterizations of Blacks, without an effort, it is difficult to see how much we (Blacks and non-Blacks) have in common. The inability to identify like qualities coupled with negative imagery and/or experience leads to group stereotyping. You typically attribute the negative characteristics of one (Black person) to the whole (Black people). And you could argue that I am doing that very thing to you right now, grouping all non-Blacks. But, while it may or may not bother you, it is definitely not life altering. For Black folks, negative attributions impact our health, well-being and general chances for success. Recognizing and correcting tendencies to pejoratively generalize is a good start to toward making things better.

In a perfect world (in the oft-recited words of Rodney King) we would just all get along. But it's human nature to gravitate to people who look like you, or in whom you see yourself positively reflected. Be that as it may, most of us cannot entirely avoid the other people who don't meet that criterion. And when interacting with "those people" is unavoidable, it shouldn't be something you dread, are <u>unreasonably</u> fearful of, or that makes you uncomfortable. In fact, it can be downright pleasant to interact with Black folks if you keep reading and learn to avoid the pitfalls addressed in this book.

Congratulations. After reading this book, old or young, liberal or conservative, White or otherwise, you'll be leaps ahead of your fellow man, appearing more confident and poised to face any Black person who crosses your path. Indeed you are brave to buy this book in this fear driven day and age. It's an acknowledgement that you don't have all the answers, but that you're are open enough to seek them out. Major props (respect) to you friend....props to you.

Introduction

First, I have to reiterate that *Why Do Black People Love Fried Chicken? And Other Questions You've Wondered But Didn't Dare Ask* is specifically about American Blacks. Throughout the text, the terms Black and African-American are used interchangeably. Perhaps it's generational, but I prefer the term Black. It works for me so I've decided to stick with it. Unfortunately (and you've probably experienced this) I've had White and Black people harass me into using African-American. I think it's supposed to be less confusing if we (Black folks) present a united front. I almost feel sorry for the people that are cowed into using African-American because it's currently politically correct. I thought everyone was okay with "Black" but apparently there was a problem and the rules were changed.

Who makes these decisions and why does everyone go along with them? And how will the next generations of Black Americans self-identify? According to utopian armchair sociologists, with all the race mixing, future generations won't require any term at all. Until then, you should recognize that within the Black community, on this and other issues, there has always been tremendous diversity of thought. As a community we are far from monolithic. We are unified in large part by the commonality of our experiences as Black Americans. If nothing else, Black folks can always bond over the experience of racism.

By now it should be clear that one Black person can't speak for all Black people – or perhaps this is not so obvious and hence the desperate need for this book. So please allow me to restate this again and as many times as is necessary. In the course of discussing certain topics in this book I will appear to be speaking for all Black people – I DO NOT. The fact is I cannot – although writing this book seems to put me in a paradoxical position.

Nevertheless, I demand the same leeway you would grant a non-Black writer. For example, I don't think you'd ever believe a non-Black writer would presume to speak for all non-Black people. However, many of you are under the false impression that there is a Black school of thought, a Black leader or a way to be Black that can be gleaned from a person or a book. And unfortunately, while answering questions I'll appear guilty of supporting these very notions. However, I can only emphasize again, and hope you come to understand, that neither I nor any other person speaks for all Black people. Having said that, as a Black person, I can set you on the right track with regard to those questions you're too scared or ashamed to ask. It's really too bad that you would be either of those things, but given the current state of affairs, it is entirely understandable.

These days, it is far more popular to be self-congratulatory about how far we've come than to suggest that there might be a breach in American race relations. Admitting the problem begs the question, what can we do and what are we willing to do about it? People are understandably reluctant to have any conversation about race. Any misstatement or explicit expression of derision towards Black individuals, life, or culture can land you in serious trouble. However, when those intentionally or accidentally offensive parties are silenced, we lose the opportunity for an honest dialogue.

People walk a fine and uncertain line with regard to conversations about race. For instance, former U.S. Secretary of Education William Bennett made a statement on his radio show about aborting all Black babies to decrease the crime rate. He explained that his statement was taken out of context. He was arguing against the practicality of such extreme measures, but not their potential efficacy. Fred DeBerry, 22-year veteran coach of the U.S. Air Force Academy football team, suggested in an interview that his team needs more minority players ("Afro-Americans…who run extremely well"). He eventually apologized for his statement, probably under the threat of termination. And let us not forget Bill Cosby, currently on a lecture circuit, clarifying his initially scathing public comments about Black folks (also taken out of context, I'm sure).

Those are three very different circumstances with the same outcome. The lesson is not to initiate any race-based statements because no one is safe from chastisement. Given this current stance, there can be no progress toward a healthy model of race relations. Pretending there are no problems means things remain the same. And while these types of statements slip in and out of the public consciousness, the lingering aftereffects place a chill on race relations. Right now we (Blacks and Whites) live with the dulled acceptance that that's just the way things are.

I don't expect this book to abolish racism, racist thoughts, or racist actions any more than the thousands of other books on race relations. But I am hopeful that someone will take these words and purposefully decide it's time to speak honestly about their true feelings and behaviors. Ultimately it is people who can change the strained personal relations interactions and institutionalized unjust practices in our society. And initially it is one person and one action at a time.

So, what makes a person Black? Is it behavior, speech or cultural identification by any person? Determining who is Black can be likened to that famous quote about recognizing pornography; you know it when you see it. So while you see Colin Powell as Black, as a first generation American born of Jamaican parents he probably self-identifies as West Indian. In fact, you should know that many people from Caribbean countries that appear "Black" do not consider themselves Black per se (due to negative cultural connotations) and sometimes go out of their way to distinguish themselves from Black Americans. This is not without merit because culturally speaking; there can be major differences between Black Americans and Caribbean Blacks (West Indians). But back to the question, what makes a person Black?

As Teresa Heinz-Kerry and her handlers were fond of saying, she is indeed African-American. But I don't think she (or you) would call her Black. Additionally, I have a Mexican friend who insists on referring to dark-skinned Latinos as Black. He is referring only to the color of their skin (darker than his fair skin) and not intending to attach the taint that goes along with being a Black American. Apparently, much like beauty, Black is in the eye of the beholder. And the designation is important because typically it's more stain than badge of honor.

In America, thoughts of Black folks bring to mind a whole host of images and sometimes visceral reactions (think Hurricane Katrina). Stop for a minute and picture a Black male. You were likely flooded with images congruent with whatever meaning you have attached to Black men. I can confidently predict that your visual was not positive because in America we've all been conditioned by basically the same negative words and images. It's sad but this conditioning is so ingrained that even most Black folks would conjure similar images.

I have known many dark-skinned immigrants who are shocked as they come to understand that in America they are perceived negatively because of their skin color – regardless of their country of origin, ancestral condition, present actions or successes. In other words, they are stigmatized as American Blacks due to the color of their skin. As a result, most people of color who could be mistaken for Black quickly learn the importance of distinguishing themselves from those who are indeed Black (Americans). Failure to do so can mean the difference between acceptance and outright hostile rejection. And while that may sound overly dramatic, this type of distinction can significantly impact one's ability to freely pursue life, liberty, and happiness.

Before going any further, I have to say something about the elephant in the room – SLAVERY. You knew this was coming and there will be more later. Now, about slavery – you can't expect Black folks to simply "get over" something that they live the ramifications of on a daily basis. As Americans (Black and White) slavery is <u>our</u> legacy, it's what birthed modern day racism. Because Blacks are easily (if not erroneously) identified as descendants of slaves by virtue of their skin color, they are thought by some (even if unconsciously) to be second-class citizens or outright inferior beings. [This would be an ideal time to discuss the inherent privilege of being born White. Instead, for an in depth analysis of White privilege I strongly recommend reading any book by Tim Wise.] In 21st Century America Blacks are incomprehensibly still treated in a manner reflective of the status of their ancestors. Just consider what happens to Black folks today: shootings of unarmed men, women, and children, lynching, handcuffing of children, racial profiling, unequal sentencing practices, etc. Irrespective of the past, it's difficult to acknowledge the extent of our progress (as a nation) without feeling like you're conceding defeat to the undesirable status quo. And in spite of things being the way are it is truly amazing (or appalling depending on your viewpoint) that any of us (Black or White) appear to have "gotten over it".

I believe there exists a certain level of resentment between Blacks and Whites because more people are not up in arms about the current state of affairs. To be uninformed is one thing, but for the vast majority who sees and turns a blind eye, it's unconscionable. From satisfied middle and upper class Blacks to Whites simply reaping the privilege of their skin color, we are all complicit to some degree. However, no matter how outraged Blacks may be, <u>alone</u> we've never had the power to effect any real change in society. The abolition of slavery and the Civil Rights Movement happened because people joined with Blacks having decided that things had to change. It seems that the spirit of dissent and speaking up for what is right is missing in America. War is definitely being waged on Black folks, and mostly it feels like we're in it alone. The marches, protests, and civil disobedience still take place because they are still necessary.

So why the seemingly blatant disregard for the lack of parity in our society? Perhaps it's that slavery thing again. Black folks are a living, breathing reminder of slavery and what it has pervasively bred – racial inequality. Slavery and its legacy are issues no one wants to think about let alone talk about. The indigenous people of this country (referred to as Native Americans) were deceived and banished to such an extent that we are no longer confronted with their decimation. Out of sight, out of mind. Because indigenous people are rarely seen or spoken of, there is no sense of responsibility or feeling that steps should be taken to rectify past injustices that impact them to this day. However, "they" haven't been able to get rid of Black folks that easily. Out of sheer determination, Blacks are still in the picture and constantly seeking reparations. Unfortunately, the outlook is bleak and at the rate we're going, American Blacks are edging ever closer to extinction. You think I exaggerate? Look at the facts: the number of men in prison, a low rate of reproduction, high rates of HIV infection, AIDS, lack of access and inferior health care, Black on Black crime, etc.

On the bright side, our plight provides you an opportunity (what else is new?). When planning your next vacation, you can save thousands of dollars and learn something in the process. Right here, in your own backyard (so to speak), you can broaden your horizons by becoming intimately familiar with a foreign culture–the last of the Black Americans. Learn our customs, taste our cuisine, and discover our historic and artistic contributions. By venturing into your local enclave of Black folks, for a fraction of the cost, you can almost certainly count on experiencing the same sort of ostracism you would in say…France. Instantly recognized as a tourist you'll be stared at, you can purchase items not found locally, you'll be puzzled by the language, and generally interact as uncomfortably as you would with any other people with whom you are unfamiliar. Don't say we never did anything for you.

And now, what you really came for – the Answers.

QUICKIES
(Yes/No Answers)

Yes - we tan/sunburn

No - that's not all my real hair

No - you can't touch my hair

No - we don't all dance/sing well or have athletic ability

Yes - some of us can swim

No - all the men aren't all well hung (but enough are that this persists to the benefit of those who are not)

I.
THE BASICS
(America's Most Wanted)

1. Is everything related to slavery?

Yes and thanks for asking. No group in America has had as poor a start as the first Africans. You'll argue that other groups had to suffer indignities and even slavery, but I immediately remind you that they migrated (i.e. came by choice). Africans were wrenched (even if purchased) from their homeland, brutalized and forced to work for free. The only way God-fearing settlers could justify the inhumane treatment of Africans was by recognizing them as 3/5ths beings in need of salvation. And of course there were the heavily relied upon economic benefits. As a result of that history, Blacks, once emancipated, have had to contend with the legacy of being thought inferior and inhuman for over 300 years.

Now, given that kind of history we're all supposed to have simply gotten over generations of conditioning... without really ever acknowledging what took place. Black people are made to feel ridiculous when we refer to the residual psychological effects, and you're not supposed to feel anything because it had nothing to do with you personally. This approach is not working for either of us.

Yes, I am aware that many White people were indentured in America. You didn't know? (Read *How the Irish Became White* by Noel Ignatiev) Were those your or your friends' ancestors? Are you able to tell by looking at them? Are any vestiges of that enslavement operative today? Alternately, you assume that the ancestors of every Black person were slaves. To many, whether consciously or not, our skin color is an indication of our roots (pun intended) and consequent status in society. So yes everything is related to slavery, if only as an ugly distant relation.

2. Is everything attributable to racism?

Well not everything, but this goes back to the slavery question (see Question #1). Slavery did not simply deprive people of freedom for free labor. Slavery promoted a doctrine of White supremacy that has outlasted the end of slavery all these years later. In short, slavery and racism, as we experience it, are inextricably joined.

3. Why are Blacks so quick to cry racism (play the race card)?

We play the race card because given our history, oftentimes it's difficult to know when it's appropriately played. You can't imagine the stress of constantly analyzing situations through the *Black Filter*. The *Black Filter* is the device through which we examine incoming information and circumstances and make determinations of motivation based thereon. For example, wondering in a given situation: is it because I'm Black, or is this person simply having a bad day? Through the *Black Filter* we attempt to determine: is it racist behavior, or a simple misunderstanding? Many of our interactions are colored by race and you have a similar process at work. When dealing with Black people you cautiously approach situations hoping they won't be misconstrued, or that some bit of prejudice won't slip out causing you to be judged and/or feel guilty. And that is why the race card is such an effective tool – unacknowledged White guilt.

While I've never had occasion to use it, the race card can come in pretty handy. As far as I can tell, almost any respectable individual can be manipulated by a charge of racism. We've all seen it happen and it's a shame because it's not always true.

4. Can't Black people be racist too?

No. Of the many definitions of racism, most require that the racist be in a position of power/influence or that they have an innate sense of superiority based on race. Blacks have never been in a significant position of power over any other group. Okay, so based on the latter requirement, I guess there could be Black folks walking around thinking they're of superior stock. Do they have the power to do anything about it? No. Ask that of your ethnic group. I think many of you (White people) don't realize just how good you got it [Second recommendation to read any book by Tim Wise re: White privilege]. The world we live in reinforces notions of White superiority and consequently confers privilege, simply for being White – lucky you!

Here's a little something for you to mull over, standard practice for Black folks.

On Being Black – Reality Check

When was the last time YOU:

Were careful of what you said in mixed company because you knew your words would represent every person who looks like you?

Were asked to provide an opinion for every person who shares your skin color?

Questioned whether you would be accepted in the neighborhood of your choice?

Questioned whether general negative personal interactions were based on the color of your skin (e.g. extended waits for service or denied entry or access (even Oprah knows this feeling))?

5. Aren't Black people prejudiced too?

Absolutely! I am shocked this comes as a surprise. Everyone indulges in pre-judging and stereotyping. I think the actual question is whether we can be racists (see Question #4).

6. Do Blacks deserve reparations?

The way many Black folks see it, Native Americans were in small part recompensed for the injustice done them, the Japanese were remunerated for their internment, and Jews are still receiving monies owed to them from people who benefited from the Holocaust, including the U.S. government. So why not the ancestors of those indentured for over 300 years?

In case there's still a doubt in your mind, perhaps this will persuade you:

TOP 5 REASONS FOR REPARATIONS
(in reverse order)

5. Other groups have received reparations, why shouldn't we?

4. Perhaps many of us would decide to move to Africa, or set up our own little spot of land where you could keep an eye on us – from afar of course.

3. Our ancestors slaved for free laying the foundation for this fine country – what's fair is fair: past due wages plus interest.

2. It would be good for the economy. Imagine how quickly any cash payments would flood the retail market (cars, jewelry, and sneakers for everyone).

1. Wouldn't it be worth it to shut us up on the slavery issue once and for all?

7. Why do Blacks try to act White?

The prevailing culture in America is White, a fact never fully examined because it benefits the prevailing culture. By the way, exactly what is White culture? Anyway, back to why Blacks try to act White. Assimilation is the stated goal for Blacks just as it is for all minority groups in America. The more we're like you, the less trouble we'll cause and the more comfortable you'll feel around us. Some Blacks wholeheartedly buy into this idea ("acting White") believing it will increase their level of acceptance.

8. Why are Blacks always trying to separate themselves?

Don't take it personally. Remember my earlier theory about the impending extinction of Black folks (see Introduction), remaining separate is, in part, about self-preservation. By not fully assimilating, we are able to retain parts of ourselves that cannot be touched.

Some Black folks go far out of their way to separate and avoid being like you. This is particularly true of those upon whom you heap the most scorn – you know, the "ghetto types." Their motto is the more dissimilar or abrasive the better and a lot of it is by design. Besides, you should be glad we keep a part of ourselves separate; it nurtures and sustains our creativity. From a place of separateness, we create a new dance, you copy, a new style of music, you copy, a new word or way of speaking…you copy. You should thank God that in America that old pot has never fully melted.

9. Why have Blacks failed when other minorities have prospered?

Is this a model minority vs. Blacks question? Well, without getting into a lengthy explanation (or making excuses) I'll simply refer you to Question #1.

Furthermore, this is another instance where Blacks are judged as a group, this time of underachievers, rather than being considered for our individual achievements. We count Oprah, P-Diddy, Condoleezza

Rice, Robert Johnson and plenty of athletes among our successful. These people can't be used for and against us. In other words, either we've made it or not. And finally, by what standard are we judged unsuccessful? Remember that just as each person listed above is successful in his/her own right, success means different things to different people.

10. Why are Blacks so paranoid?

We are paranoid based on history, experience, and the ongoing need to pass our perceptions through the **Black Filter** (see Question #3). As a non-Black person, you would never expect that your skin color might hinder or prevent equal treatment. For example, in 1972 the federal government finally conceded that for forty years (between 1932 and 1972), the U.S. Public Health Service conducted an experiment on 399 Black men in the late stages of syphilis. By the end of the experiment, 28 of the men had died directly of syphilis, 100 were dead of related complications, 40 of their wives had been infected, and 19 of their children had been born with congenital syphilis. In essence these men were human guinea pigs. It's probably difficult for you to accept that the U.S. government deliberately allowed a group of its citizens to die from a terrible disease. Conversely, newly informed Black people would not be at all surprised because this is not the only documented incident of its kind. And because Blacks know what our government is capable of, it's easier for conspiracy theories (e.g. surrounding AIDS or Hurricane Katrina) to gain traction in the community. At long last, many other Americans are awakening to the truth about the U.S. government. So now who's paranoid?

11. Why are Blacks so sneaky/lazy?

In part, the paranoia addressed in the previous answer is the reason for what you perceive as sneaky or clandestine behavior. Many Black people have learned to always be on guard and that operating under the radar keeps them from being targeted. So it's entirely possible that what you interpret as sneaky/lazy could simply be action of which you're unaware.

Additionally, Blacks have been seduced (some would say more than average) by the Siren song of consumerism. However, having recognized that success may not be accessible on the standard path, the flip side of traditional hard work is hustling. Although hustling happens behind the scenes, you shouldn't take it as lazy or the easy way out. It's the difference between being an employee and an entrepreneur. As a hustler (entrepreneur), it may not always be legal and is potentially lucrative, but if you don't work, you don't eat.

As a final response to this question, there are those Black people who feel entitled to the ongoing government support to which they've become accustomed. There's a victim syndrome at work that no amount of assistance (financial or otherwise) can ever hope to overcome. Now we can agree, that's lazy.

12. How come Blacks come in so many colors?

I am answering this question with respect to Black Americans. We come in so many colors because of... slavery. African-Americans (if that's the term of your choosing) don't exist without the forced (or coerced) sexual interaction between Africans (slaves) and early-

Americans. Of course once in America, Africans and African-Americans also mixed with indigenous and other immigrants. Sometimes you'll hear Black Americans proudly proclaim or deny that they are of mixed race. Well, now you can boldly inform them – all Blacks are mixed. It's just a matter of how far back you go.

13. Why are there so many Black professional athletes?

There are so many because of the genetic gifts with which many (but not all) of us are blessed. Why (in addition to racism) do you think we were shut out of sports for so long? For an in-depth analysis of this issue, please read *Taboo: Why Black Athletes Dominate Sports and Why We're Afraid to Talk About It* by Jon Entine. For many young Blacks, seeing is believing. It follows that if the majority of people dominating a sport look like you (and you're predisposed to succeed), you're more likely to give it a go. This is exemplified by the overwhelming desire of Black youths to become rappers and athletes with far fewer pursuing swimming and the sciences.

These guys learned the hard way about the taboo of talking race and sports. And now sports fans, introducing the:

FOOT IN MOUTH ALL-STARS
(In no particular order):

Jimmy the Greek, former sports broadcaster referring to Black athletes as being "…bred to be the better athlete because, this goes all the way to the Civil War when …

the slave owner would breed his big woman so that he would have a big black kid. "

Larry Cochell, former Oklahoma baseball coach praised a Black baseball player by saying "…he has no nigger in him."

Al Campanis, former Dodgers general manager said, "[Blacks]) may not have some of the necessities to be, let's say, a field manager, or perhaps a general manager."

Paul Hornung, said Notre Dame needed to lower its academic standards to "get the black athlete." "We can't stay as strict as we are as far as the academic structure is concerned because we've got to get the black athlete…" and finally,

Fuzzy Zoeller, said after Tiger Woods won the Masters, "You pat him on the back and say congratulations and enjoy it and tell him not to serve fried chicken next year. Got it?" and added, "or collard greens or whatever the hell they serve."

14. Isn't it progress when we adopt Black ways of speaking, dressing, etc.?

No, it most definitely is <u>not</u> progress. Moreover, many Blacks find it insulting, particularly the speech mimicry. And what exactly would your imitation be progress towards? And progress for whom? It does not draw us nearer culturally and certainly doesn't give you any greater empathy for the plight of Black folks. It doesn't indicate that either of us have overcome our conditioning or improve relations. Forgive me if I fail to see the forward movement for Black people. It must feel progressive for you to step into the cultural fun house for a time... but we live there. Stepping in and out of your cultural identity is a privilege of your skin color. [Again, I strongly recommend reading any book by Tim Wise.].

BEST LOVED/HONORARY BLACK PEOPLE
(In no particular order):

Jesus, Bill Clinton, Eminem, Quentin Tarantino, Rick Rubin, Justin Timberlake (pre-Janet) and Paul Wall

15. Do we need a full month dedicated to Black history?

Yes. It would take innumerable years of annual remembrances to instill in you the significant contributions of every other group of Americans. The (simpleton) opposing argument is that we should also have White History Month. Come now, every month of K-12 History is dedicated to the contributions of "White" people. As a result, many of you believe that anything worth knowing was done or created by White people.

So really, it comes down to you being horribly under-educated. Most minorities are not only educated in "American" history, but also about the history of their respective peoples. You should use Black History Month as an opportunity to round out your education. And just so everyone knows, this educational period started out as a week. It grew to the month of February because it's the birth month of Abraham Lincoln and statesman Frederick Douglass, not because it's the shortest month of the year.

HOW BLACKS HAVE CHANGED/ IMPROVED YOUR LIFE:

Rock and Roll. Without the combination of gospel and the Blues (which you're responsible for us having) you'd still be two-stepping to country. Africans brought with them a rhythmic approach to music unlike the tonal/melodic approach of the early settlers. Can you think rock and roll without Chuck Berry, Little Richard or Bo Diddley? Well, you shouldn't.

Elvis/Eminem. These guys would have had no one to emulate and generations of you wouldn't have been able to rebel from your parents by acting out against the mainstream; AND

Drug Use. Your drug use, traffic violations, or any other criminal activities would be much more readily detectable if the police were not so focused on pursuing, stopping, and rousting Black people.

Where's the love?

16. What makes a person Black?

Part of the answer is simple. Since race is a social construct, technically you could just start referring to yourself as Black and see if it catches on – if people accept it then it's so. Be that as it may, there is a lot of history behind this question and hence a lot of confusion.

At one time in America, one drop of Black blood was enough to consider a person Black (that's one powerful drop). Nowadays, with so much mixing, things are a little more complicated. While some groups are very invested in maintaining a strict distinction, it's not always possible on sight to tell who is Black. Is it enough to be culturally Black, Black because you identify as such, Black if you look it or Black when it's convenient (see below)? Why is this so important…for the census count, congressional reapportionment or media polls?

OH NO YOU DIDN'T!
(Statements actually made to me):

You're not Black enough for me, I don't consider you to be Black, You're not like them (other Blacks) and you're not really Black.

Note to self: Must try harder!

17. Why are Black people always claiming other people as Black?

Some Blacks claim notable people as Black (e.g. Tiger Woods) because it gives them someone to feel proud of, even if those same people reject them. You have to wonder why certain actors (e.g. Vin Diesel) won't even admit that there is Black in their bloodline (there's that one drop thing again). Is it for fear of being typecast or stigmatized? On the other hand, admittedly bi-racial Halle Berry (African-American/White) totally identifies as Black, we all see her as Black and she accepted her Oscar for Black actresses and other nameless women of color. The story here was that a Black woman won, not a bi-racial woman. I wonder how her White mother feels, basically having her entire contribution negated. Society places people in such a strange situation – choose or be chosen for. I guess it's nice (or confusing) for those who have a choice, but it's terrible have to choose.

18. Why don't Blacks just go back to Africa?

Yes, people still ask this one. Anyway, the answer is why would we? Most of us have never been and have no known ties. Secondly, thanks to your ancestors, our ancestors have been here for almost as long as yours (you know, that slavery thing again). Once there was a chance to repatriate the Africans but that time has long since passed. And finally, studies show that we're probably related somewhere down the line. Now you wouldn't banish a distant relative to a foreign land would you – yeah, given the chance you just might.

19. Aren't Blacks better off than if they were in Africa?

Who knows, Africa is a big place most of us know only through what we see on television. And I assume we are considering modern day Africa after having been blighted by years of colonial rule, slavery, and the ongoing theft of natural resources? In the U.S., we're conditioned to quantify material success as a major factor of happiness. Having constantly measured life by that standard, I can see where people would be quick to agree that Americans are better off. And don't get me wrong, I feel blessed to have been born in the U.S. and to enjoy our freedoms. However, even with all we have, Americans are not the happiest people in the world (in fact I believe we're 15th according to the World Values Survey). So ultimately, I guess better off is a relative notion and it all depends upon whom you ask.

20. Why do Black people love fried chicken and watermelon?

A lot of Black people love fried chicken and watermelon for the same reason that other people love them, they taste good. Here's my theory: many Black folks have their roots in the South where the frying of chicken was raised to a fine art. Much of what is called soul food (including fried chicken) is made up of Southern foods tweaked by Black folks. But while popular with many, fried chicken, watermelon, and the love of them have been <u>negatively</u> connected with Black people through years of caricatures. The association is so strong that fried chicken is practically Black America's national food. Goodness knows the bird flu is going to be especially hard on Black folks. Luckily I don't eat fried chicken (can't stand the skin); but watermelon and me…that's a different story.

Ready, set, go!!

Once upon a time, a naive young Black girl (yours truly) was enjoying her jr. high school picnic. She was the only Black girl in her class but it was okay because… well, no one had made an issue about it.

After the egg toss and sack races, there was a watermelon eating contest. The young Black girl signed up immediately without giving it a second thought. She had always been fiercely competitive, loved watermelon, and had already won a few other ribbons that day. Plus it was a hot day and…she really loved watermelon. Finally it was time. She and the other contestants lined up in front of their portions. "Ready, set, go!!"

It was over before it started. The other students never stood a chance against the hyper-competitive watermelon eating machine. She proudly accepted and wore her First Place Ribbon the rest of the day.

In hindsight, this story is hilarious – now that I get it. I recall that particular ribbon ceremony felt strange and was funny to the adults (and some children). Sure, it's possible they were laughing about something else; but picture a lone Black child at a table full of White kids plowing through chunks of watermelon at warp speed – for a ribbon. I had no idea my inbred insatiable hunger for watermelon would permit me to effortlessly bury the competition. Since the adults knew of my advantage, I really shouldn't have been allowed to compete; it just wasn't fair to the other kids.

This brings to mind an important question. Where should Black children go to learn about all the stereotypes they will be saddled with for the rest of their lives, thereby avoiding these types of scenarios?

II.
SPEECH
(Axe Me Again and
I'll Tell You the Same)

A Black person's way of speaking is definitely a nurture (and not nature) issue. In other words, Black people are not born speaking English with a **Blackccent** (a characteristic way of speaking English that allows you, sight unseen, to identify people as Black). Of course, the major problem with identification by Blackccent is that all you can really tell is whether a person matches what you believe a Black person sounds like.

Nevertheless, the notion of choice with respect to speech is much easier to grasp now than it was in the past. That's because these days, so many non-Blacks speak with a Blackccent. In fact, I challenge you to make it through a day without your Blackccent. You may think it's only about slang, but it's also about inflection and usage. For better or worse (depending upon whom you ask), the cultural landscape has been saturated with Blackccented English. It's kind of like saying "patio" without realizing you're speaking another language (Spanish) or using a word ("picnic") that has a foreign derivation (French). The unique ways Blacks use words are so deeply entrenched in American culture (and abroad) that they are thought of as Standard English.

Here's a simple example of usage: "baby got *back*" (referring to an ample rear end), "I've got your *back*" (you can count on me), "*back* up off me" (give me some space or else) versus the standard use "please step *back*" (move backwards).

Like you, most Black people know when and where it's appropriate (or necessary) to lapse into the Blackccent. Oprah's speech is frequently peppered with Blackccented English in order to communicate warmth and familiarity. Thanks(?) to Oprah, many people have become (too) comfortable with adopting the Blackccent.

However, that is not to say that all Black people move easily between Blackccented and Standard English. Since Standard English was primarily spoken in my home, my Blackccent has only been cultivated as an adult. As a result, for many years, Black people taunted me for not having it. And now, strangely enough, occasionally even non-Blacks reject me as "not Black enough" – see below. Frankly, I still haven't mastered a Blackccent. Nonetheless, I wouldn't dare try to fake it. That is something that rarely goes over well and usually comes across as condescending. I only wish more non-Blacks would adopt my position on this point.

21. Why is it okay for Blacks to call each other *nigger* but not okay for other people?

Even Black folks get caught up in this debate amongst themselves. First of all, Black people are not calling each other nig<u>ger</u>. Secondly, your fully annunciated use of the word (emphasis on the "er") is the dead giveaway of your unease with the word and a sign you shouldn't use it. Thirdly, if you want to know why your use (as opposed to ours) is such a big deal, there is a book entitled *Nigger: The Strange Career of a Troublesome Word* by Randall Kennedy that provides the entire history of the word and its use. Finally, my favorite response to this question is a question. Knowing the history of this word, why would <u>you</u> want to call us nigger or any variation thereof? And if after all that you still wonder why, I can only say: it's a Black thing – and you wouldn't understand.

A Story About How Using The "N" Word Can Go Horribly Wrong:

I have a non-Black friend that I have known for over 20 years. I met her in junior high school where I was one of three Black people and we've had regular contact to the present day. I hope I've conveyed that this woman is no stranger to me.

About three years ago we were talking about her new job in Georgia where's she's been living for many years now. While recounting her day (and without missing a beat) she told me that she had to clear a bunch of *niggers* out of a building where they were squatting. Even though I had never heard her use the word, it wasn't so much that she referred to those Black people as niggers. I was more stunned that she felt comfortable using the word to me – especially since I had never used the word around her.

The ease with which it came out of her mouth told me that it wasn't the first time she had used it. It's one thing for her to have felt comfortable with her "Black friend" (which she shouldn't have), but it made me wonder how frequently she referred to Blacks in this manner in the course of conversation with others. Of course I asked her to explain what she meant and after some fumbling, she did. Admittedly, it rocked our friendship a bit, but <u>we talked about it.</u> And maybe she still freely uses *nigger* with other friends, but at least now she knows it's not okay to use around me.

Trust me on this, even when your Black friends assure you that your use of *nigger* is okay with them, it is constantly being vetted through the **Black Filter** (see Question #3) for context and intent. Be careful, one slip up could mean big problems. Better yet, don't use it at all.

22. Why do Black people greet each other in odd ways (e.g. the handshake, my nigga', etc.)?

These greetings demonstrate a level of familiarity and warmth between the exchanging parties. They can also acknowledge a bond that is neither dictated by nor limited to skin color. An example is when Black folks refer to each other (or others) as brother or sister – when clearly we're not all related. Having said all that, I think the primary reason these greetings persist is because Blacks find conventional ways of interacting, including speech, to be stiff and formal so we've adapted them more to our liking.

23. Why do Blacks always acknowledge each other?

Acknowledging other Black folks helps to establish a level of comfort when there aren't that many of us around specifically (in the room) and generally (in numbers).

Based on skin color, we (sometimes) erroneously assume that if nothing else, we share the negative experience of being Black Americans (see Introduction re: who is Black). However, all Blacks are not Black Americans and neither have they shared the same experiences. Black American experience ranges from debutantes to thug life and everything in between. So occasionally I might send out a friendly nod and get nothing in return – no recognition, just glazed eyes. And if you presume you'd recognize a "Black" person on sight, I'd love to be there for your first encounter with a dark-skinned Spanish speaking Afro-Latino.

24. Why do Black people talk trash all the time?

It's an excellent way to psyche yourself up and your opponent out. Additionally, trash talking has become extremely lucrative. Let's take rapping for example. In the beginning, rap was all about trash talk and who could spit the best game at the expense of the other guy (battle rapping). It's likely that many rappers got their start playing the dozens (what you call snapping) in the neighborhood. It takes a certain verbal dexterity, but it is not exclusive to Black folks. Nevertheless, Black folks have taken it, and trash talk in general, to another level. What, in addition to his athletic ability, made Muhammad Ali (channeling Jack Johnson) so special? It was his constant flow of bluster, which he always backed up. And now we have Kanye West using the same techniques to advance his favorite cause – himself. I can't blame him for reviving a good thing. It gets him a lot of attention.

25. Why do Black people talk to the movie screen?

I'm also puzzled by this one. It's rude and outright annoying. I often wonder if these Black folks are aware that their behavior is socially inappropriate and just don't give a damn. Although, I have to admit I'm not completely unfamiliar with this behavior. I've done my fair share of screaming at the television news – in the privacy of my own home. That's before I realized I could simply change the channel. Be honest, you've done it too. I guess there's just an oddball percentage of the population for whom every show, public or otherwise, means audience participation time ala Rocky Horror Picture Show.

26. Why do Blacks speak improper English?

Some Black folks speak what is variously called Ebonics or Black English because it was spoken in the home and/or neighborhood where they were raised. They may or may not have the ability to speak what you regard as Standard English. On the other hand, it could simply be a lack of desire. It is much more important for them to maintain favor with their peer group than with those whom they are unconcerned (i.e. you). Our whole lives, Blacks are taught that assimilation is the way to get ahead. For some, speaking Standard English is seen as a big step towards the undesirable end that is complete assimilation. Fortunately, there are some Black folks who work to preserve their identity and/or separateness (see Question #8) in speech, among other ways, sometimes just to confound you.

HOW TO AVOID LOOKING FOOLISH WHEN "TALKING BLACK"

This is a really easy one...don't do it. But since I know you won't heed this advice, just remember: the "ghetto" slang lexicon changes frequently (see urbandictionary.com). It changes so regularly that I don't dare attempt to *put you up* (update you) on the latest. However, I can give you a good rule of thumb. Once you hear certain words or phrases bandied about by the mainstream media or in commercials, they're officially over. That means you continue to use them at the risk of appearing foolish.

Let's take a moment to reflect on some phrases you've overused into uncool oblivion:

"Don't go there," "you go girl," "my bad," "don't be a hater," "bling, bling," etc.

And oh yes, you should definitely rely on friends and family to let you know when you've gone too far. Heed their advice – they love you. Those encouraging your usage are either as uncool as you, or are mocking you behind your back.

27. Is Ebonics a language?

Ebonics, also known as Black English or African-American Vernacular English, is a dialect of American English. It's a way of speaking characteristic of some Black folks.

By definition, Klingon (Star Trek) and Elvish (Lord of the Rings) are true languages. However, unlike Ebonics (currently experiencing a troubling resurgence among non-Blacks) neither language is in wide circulation. Even so, if you tried really hard, like Ebonics, you could also master Klingon or Elvish. Of course, the downside is that you'll find it difficult to integrate into daily life. On top of that, you will most definitely be mocked and shunned for your use. It's your choice.

28. Why do Blacks speak one way to Blacks and differently to non-Blacks?

I have come to think of Black folks as bilingual – Black English (Blackccent) /Standard English. Blind studies have shown that ethnicity can be determined through speech inflections (they needed a study?). It has also been demonstrated that speech-identified Blackness can decrease prospects for employment, housing, or perceptions of intelligence.

The reason Blacks occasionally speak with a Blackccent is because it is required to move in and out of different social circles. Sometimes I look at it like a game. While my regular speech is almost entirely devoid of a Blackccent, on the phone I occasionally play it up for fun, at your expense. At the revelation of my Blackness, the shocked expressions are sometimes entertaining but mostly they're predictably annoying. It lets me know you have a very limited perception of Black people. Not all Black people speak with a Blackccent. And if we're capable of changing up, we're also able to discern when use of the Blackccent is appropriate. Geez, give us some credit.

III.
MEDIA
(What You See
Is Not What You Get)

Where to begin? The most important point to communicate is that media is a business. As such, it is managed to produce a profit. We may know this as a fact but we seldom consider it as we watch movies, television or news programming. In order to have the broadest appeal, media characterizations are frequently consistent with our preconceived ideas, otherwise they seem unbelievable to us. In other words, television for example, primarily reinforces what we already believe to be true. And unfortunately this is where you get and reaffirm most of your ideas about Black people.

Since there is so much money to be made, I understand why Black people are willing to "pimp" themselves out in the public eye, seemingly without regard for the consequences. But this is no victimless crime. As a result of exaggerated media portrayals, many Blacks feel forced to defend the race against stereotypical images all the while resenting the burden of having to do so. Some Blacks also defend their right to buffoonery by saying: "don't hate the player, hate the game" – and I am inclined to agree, to an extent. While the individual players should not be absolved from their bad behavior, they are merely pawns in the overall scheme. Those Black folks rarely have any ownership or say in how they are portrayed.

Put another way, those ever-present negative cultural influences you feel powerless to protect your family from (e.g. hip-hop culture) are NOT controlled by Blacks. For example, Sumner Redstone (not a Black man) controls Viacom whose holdings include Paramount, MTV, VH-1, CBS, BET, Nickelodeon, CBS, Infinity Broadcasting, Blockbuster Video and book publisher Simon & Schuster. Right there is your weekly entertainment line-up. Even traditional purveyors of Black culture Motown, Essence Magazine and Africana. com, among others, are owned by non-Blacks. Perhaps if we made it clear to the Redstones of the world that we do not approve of the status quo, we might see a change. And that includes Black people too.

29. Why is the Black person always the first to die in movies?

It could be art imitating life; we all know that Black folks are easily dispensable. Additionally, knocking off the Black character is now a successful Hollywood formula. The happy ending, the good guy gets the girl, the hooker with the heart of gold, and the Black guy gets it first – all time tested Hollywood traditions. Since there was a time when Blacks weren't allowed in the movie at all, I think we're supposed to be grateful for the opportunity to be the first knocked off.

30. Why is there a television station for Black people (B.E.T.)?

Black people need their own media outlets to be able to widely disseminate images that accurately depict them. Not all of those images will be positive because that's not reality. However, <u>the idea</u> is to have the ability to control media content so that the message is not predominately negative. The presumption is that a Black person would have a vested interest in balanced broadcasting. Unfortunately, I can't say that was the case with former B.E.T. owner Robert L. Johnson (a Black man). Anyway, it's a moot point now because he sold B.E.T. to media mogul Sumner Redstone (not a Black man).

And since some of you are thinking it, having White Entertainment Television is like having White History Month. The vast majority of television is White entertainment television, programmed to appeal to the majority of Americans.

31. What happened between Omarosa and Kwame on *The Apprentice*?

To briefly recap, this was a case of a Black person double-cross. In a critical situation (where a $250,000 salary was at stake), Kwame unwisely chose to align himself based on race rather than professional ability. That's always the wrong choice, but particularly when he had so much to lose. Poor Kwame was blinded by Omarosa's skin color and viper-like seductive charm, which she turned on and off at will.

Now in fairness to her, the Omarosa type – "angry Black woman" is a popular formulaic reality television characterization. Of course, Omarosa could actually be a lying, scheming, race baiting, attention seeker. And/or as it turns out, she was media savvy in playing to type, milking her fifteen minutes longer than any other former Apprentice? If her plan was to remain in the limelight, she has succeeded because we're not likely to forget her name; then again, she does have one of those kinds of names (see Question #43).

BE THANKFUL
FOR BLACK PEOPLE BECAUSE:

- Who else could so easily create conflict (read ratings) on reality television programs?

- Besides a well placed Black person, how else would you establish urban settings in movies and television?

- Who else can provide diversity (i.e. a token splash of color) on The Bachelor/Bachelorette (as if that person actually has a chance)?

- Without us, your perennial favorite television show COPS could not exist.

- Who would Maury Povich book for those mindlessly entertaining paternity determination shows? ("Are you my baby's daddy?")

32. Who speaks for Black people now?

Oh, you mean the Black leader (also see Question #56). Well, CNN or other major television outlets anoint the Black leader. And we (the Black community) usually find out at the same time as you who this person is, what we think and where we stand on certain issues. It's important for you to know that all Blacks don't agree with the CNN appointee. He (and it's almost always a man) is typically a sold out media whore promoting some semi-personal agenda. Not too much different from the White leader (whoever that is). I think the Black leader is mostly for the benefit of non-Black people. It's convenient to be able to get the perspective of a whole group from one person (kind of like reading this book).

At least now Black opinion is much more likely to be represented by opposite extremes (and you thought the Black Republican was a myth). Still, whenever they showcase that one guy (e.g. Alan Keys, Shelby Steele, Larry Elder, etc.) it feels disingenuous. I say it's time for a change. Hey, why not me for the next Black leader?

33. Why do racial issues always come down to Black/White concerns?

It's strange but true that when newsworthy events gain national attention, media polling only reflects the opinions of Black and White Americans. Some of it is lazy technique on the part of the pollsters. When contacting a household for a response, it's much easier to qualify self-identified Blacks and Whites than to run through all the possible classifications of Asians or Latinos, etc. Additionally, as indicated in Question #32, it's convenient to be able to get the perspective of a whole group from one easily identified person. Evidently, events of national significance do not require the input of Latinos, Asians, Pacific Islanders, Indigenous people, etc. That is sure to change over the next ten years.

On another note, how often do you see polls where the opinions of Black and White Americans are statistically close? It would be newsworthy if the polls reflected the agreement that exists on some issues. However, that would never make the broadcast because dissension makes for more interesting news.

34. What are we supposed to call Blacks now?

Are we talking in public or in private? But seriously, I understand your confusion – we've gone from "Nigger" to "Colored" to "Negro" to "Black" to "Afro-American" to "Person of Color" to "African-American"…phew. I've seen your hesitation and sensed your discomfort when in conversation it's necessary to indicate a person's race. I've even seen you correct other non-Blacks when they use a non-current word (e.g. colored). This happens more frequently at work, where social norms are strictly enforced – lest anyone cry racism.

Anyway, the truth of the matter is there's no telling what a Black person expects to hear from you, or what they might find offensive – it depends on the person. I'll allow Negro or Colored from a senior citizen, but *nigger* (or any variation thereof) is never acceptable. I suggest that you call Blacks, with conviction, whatever makes you comfortable. Even if you're wrong (if there is such a thing here), you know your intent, and if necessary you can explain yourself without hesitation. [AUTHOR NOTE: Most times your hesitation/discomfort leads me to believe you barely avoided referring to Joe Black person as a *nigger*. Something you might have otherwise done if you weren't talking to me. I'm just saying.]

IV.
STYLE/CULTURE
('Cuz You Know We Got Soul)

Do all Black people love fried chicken, Asian people rice, Jews money and Latinos spicy food? Individual minority groups are not typically educated in the school of negative stereotyping – at least not about our own group. Consequently, it may come as a surprise to your Black friend for instance, that he or she is supposed to love fried chicken, be a good dancer/athlete and have inbred criminal tendencies. It certainly would have been useful to know these things in advance; I might have spared myself some embarrassment (See story below Question # 20).

Nevertheless, I must thank my learned non-Black friends who, through their questioning, brought me up to speed on Black stereotypes. I guess that means I also have to grudgingly thank those who taught me through their prejudice. What I'm saying is don't be surprised if a Black person (depending on their age and upbringing) is clueless about what you accept as fact about them. I have been truly baffled by some of the questions people have asked me about Black folks and in turn had to them where they had gotten their information.

Speaking of questions, I have a few questions of my own. Why is it that when a White person sings, dances or plays sports like a Black person it is made out to be so remarkable? Is the level of the Black performer the standard to which all others strive? And do Blacks deserve and earn less credit because of a stereotypical expectation of excellence?

It is certainly unfair to elevate one group (non-Blacks) over another (Blacks) because the former excels at mimicry of the latter. This is a bizarre and long-standing American tradition, particularly in the artistic community. I know that imitation is supposed to be highest form of flattery but it's also nice to be appropriately credited for skill and innovation. As an example, is Joss Stone simply a phenomenon among White performers or is she a true talent among all the talented? Should she only be compared to her White counterparts or can she otherwise hold her own? Most importantly, if she were Black with her singing ability, would anyone care about Joss Stone? I think not.

Unfortunately, this never works in reverse. In other words, don't ever expect to hear a single one of the wildly talented Black rock groups (yes, they do exist – see blackrockcoalition.org) in heavy rotation on the radio or at MTV. And if you're only rebuttal has something to do with the band Living Colour, then you've made my point. There are plenty of other similar groups that will never have any commercial success. Why is that? Meanwhile, a certain marginally talented non-Black rapper generates more hype and sales than anybody, ever, and then "retires" on the top (?). I just don't get it.

Music Forms "Created" by Blacks Now More Popular with Whites

Blues
Rock and Roll
Reggae (at least in America)
Rap (I see you Brown people)
Jazz

35. What is C.P.T.?

C.P.T. is an acronym for Colored People Time. This means that if the designated meet time is 5:00 p.m., expect the Black person operating on C.P.T. to arrive anywhere from 5:30 p.m. onward. This behavior is typically exclusive of, but may encompass, being fashionably late. I've heard it explained as having one's internal clock set on "island time" as opposed to being on the Protestant work schedule. It's that laid back tempo we all adopt while on vacation. While that may be true, I think folks on C.P.T. have simply decided the time to get there is when they arrive – and to hell with everyone else. While not all Black people operate on C.P.T. I will say this, if you are attending an event hosted by Black folks, it probably won't start on time – so plan accordingly.

36. Why are Blacks so loud and aggressive?

There's no denying that many Blacks are loud and demonstrative. However, the connection of loudness with aggression is a misinterpretation of a cultural cue. In the same manner, Americans can misconstrue lack of eye contact from Asian, African or South American cultures as deceptive when it is intended to be respectful. With Black folks, being loud is simply an expression of enthusiasm (the more familiar the individual the louder) and/or volume is used for effect. Blacks hear other Blacks getting loud and scarcely bat an eye whereas non-Blacks find cause for apprehension. Of course there are soft-spoken Black people, but being loud is somewhat of a cultural norm. Increased volume can simply be about competition versus confrontation (e.g. trash talking) and/or is a way of bonding and having fun (e.g. calling each other nigga).

Alternately, Blacks use the expression "loud talking" to indicate something altogether different. To "loud talk" someone is to articulate information not meant for public consumption with the intent to embarrass. That kind of loud talking is typically provocative and can lead to aggression. Examine these variations against your views about loud speech equaling aggressive behavior. Now that you know there's a difference, in time you'll develop an ear to distinguish between talking loud (harmless) and loud talking (a potential problem).

37. Why are Black women always angry?

I've already established that Black folks can be loud and demonstrative (see Question #36), but not necessarily angry. Black women aren't always angry, but we are definitely more assertive than other American women, and that may come across as angry. Throughout history (for a myriad of reasons) Black men have been less available to protect Black women from the ills that tend to befall the fairer sex. As a result, most Black women are reared to be self-reliant, without expectation of rescue and to not accept mess from anyone. In

America, the manifestation of these traits by a female is viewed as both unfeminine and angry. Who started all that emphatic neck rolling, finger snapping and hand in the face anyway?

Real life answer: Sometimes Black women are angry for reasons having nothing to do with you. Maybe they're just having a bad day. Or it could be that they dislike and/or distrust everyone who looks like you (sound familiar?). One might even say their anger is justified given the attendant frustrations of being a Black woman in America. Or it could just be hormones, try not to take it personally.

38. Why do Black women change their hair so often?

Choice of hairstyle and color are social statements from which much can learned. We frequently alternate styles because we can (variety is the spice of life) and sometimes because we have to (e.g. at work – see Reality Check below). From traditional African braid styles to Madame C.J. Walker's (first Black female millionaire 1867-1919) straightening techniques – we've been working our 'do's for a long time. Nowadays many of these trends (weaves, extensions and braids) have become mainstream, but Black women are still the undisputed queens of the 'do'. Have you ever seen our hair shows?

And generally, a Black woman going blonde has nothing to do with trying to look White. The exception being that once you gain celebrity status, it appears mandatory to bleach your hair down to some shade of blonde. And speaking of Beyonce, *InStyle Magazine* (May, 2005) included her in a piece entitled "Stealing

Beauty." In it, Beyonce is shown having "stolen" the look of wearing cornrows from Bo Derek. Perhaps the editor is not old enough to have known any better, but the publication of this kind of silly falsehood is annoying to say the least.

On Being Black – Reality Check

When was the last time YOU:

Changed your hairstyle before a job interview (for fear of bias) knowing full well that you could change it back after being hired, without fear of termination?

Worried about finding a good place to get your hair styled because you know that the odds of finding a stylist trained on "your kind of hair" are not good?

39. Why do Black people look so young?

In a word: melanin. Melanin, a determinant in skin color, acts as a natural sunscreen for people of color. It provides a certain level of protection from the sun damage that causes your wrinkles. Nevertheless, unbeknownst to many, including Blacks, Black people do get sunburned.

40. Why do Black men love big butts?

The standard of beauty in the Black community has always been a little different from the norm. Bigger legs, breasts and butts are typically far more in demand than what is considered desirable in wider society. Black men are simply expressing appreciation for an alternate standard of beauty to which they've become accustomed. Lately Hollywood has been more successful in exporting its sickly image of beauty, but it's never really taken root in the Black community. It took Jennifer Lopez and her positive self-image (God bless her) for mainstream America to appreciate the beauty of a diverse body type. Welcome to the party. Who would have thought, non-Blacks blowing up their lips, booties and bronzing their skin? You too can have it all...for a small price.

41. Why do Black men walk the way they do?

Do you mean rhythmically with a cocksure strut as opposed to uptight, rigid, and without style? Well, I've heard that this is a hereditary remnant of being chained in slavery and having to drag more weight on one side of the body causing a delayed stagger step. That is one man's theory, but I don't buy it. The Black man's swagger is another way of advertising the goods and setting oneself apart from the pack. Between the sexes, who in the animal kingdom does all the posturing and preening? It's the male. You should be thankful that the grace and rhythm that seems lacking in many non-Blacks, comes naturally to some of us. Think about it, when is the last time a dance craze swept the nation that originated outside of Black community. And let's not forget Michael Jordan, grace personified.

42. Why do Blacks dress so flamboyantly?

Most non-European based cultures have a traditional garb that is vibrant and full of color. Contrast the traditional dress of the early Pilgrim/ Puritan with the African (and even if you believe

Africans were only clothed in animal skin – that makes my point). When they came to this country, our ancestors possessed more inherent style than could be beat out of us. It is our fashion heritage and modern-day credo: why blend in when you can stand out. So now, in the ultimate stroke of fashion irony we have rappers creating a trend by reimagining preppy-chic, all argyle and polo shirts. That's a sure way to distinguish oneself from the sea of oversized pants, shirts and jewelry that has become cliché. Keep up people.

FASHION 101

Tommy Hilfiger is smart. Once upon a time he successfully sold White people clothes to White people. Eventually they stopped wearing his clothes because they were boring (and that's saying a lot). So, he switched his focus and aligned himself with Black people, designing and marketing with them in mind. Although White people disapprovingly turned up their noses, his sales increased exponentially and he experienced a branding revival. Suddenly White people again became interested because now, Tommy Hilfiger clothes were cool Black people clothes. Tommy Hilfiger now successfully caters to both markets. Pretty slick.

43. Why do Blacks name their children those names?

Most of those name choices are related to attempts to maintain African and Afrocentric tradition. And although some of those names actually have African meanings (e.g. Imani, Aisha, Tanisha), others are creative derivations (e.g. Nashieqa). Are those names so unusual? At one time I'm sure that names like Austin, Emily and Madison seemed a little strange. Aw, who am I kidding – some of those names are hilarious and can be burdensome for the bearer. That is unless your name is Shaquille, Condoleezza or Oprah. It's quite amazing that we no longer grimace at the sound of Oprah's name, genuflect is more like it. However, I don't expect to see a future generation of Oprahs – in name.

44. Why do Blacks play their music so loud?

We play our music loud to increase our enjoyment. Okay, it's also sometimes done to piss people off, but mostly it's not about you. There's a whole car culture formed around sub-woofers, tweeters, amplifiers, and who can get the biggest sound. And here's a news flash, it's not dominated by Black people.

Makin' sweet music
Best musical products of interracial love:

Bob Marley, Alicia Keys, Sade,
Zach de la Rocha, Prince, Jimi Hendrix,
Shirley Bassey, Christina Aguilera,
Shakira, Mariah Carey

45. Why do Blacks spend so much money on things they can't afford (cars, rims, etc.)?

Living beyond one's means is hardly unique to Black people. Since even the U.S. government functions in massive debt, it's safe to say it's the American way. Some Blacks seem more fully bought into rampant consumerism for one reason: lacking a basic financial education (and doubting future prospects), they tend to purchase things with an eye on the short term. They typically associate personal worth with outward appearance – so the more attention getting, the better. Traveling about town, no one can see your investment strategy, know that you own your home or determine how much you have set aside for retirement. However, if it's flashy enough, they won't miss your car, designer clothes and jewelry. In the minds of many (especially Blacks?), you are only successful (valuable) if other people can validate you through your possessions.

46. Why do Black men always go after White women?

Textbook answer: In our society Eurocentric features are prized and consequently White women are the idealized beauty image. We have all been subjected to a lifetime of conditioning directing us to be attracted to (if you're a man) and aspire to (if you're a woman) that look.

Real life answer: Frequently there is a mutual attraction derived from curiosity (forbidden fruit) about the unknown. These are standard impulses unnaturally encouraged by the mythologized Black buck, his big penis, and more recently, White girls gone wild. Additionally, many Black men believe that a White woman will treat them better, accept worse treatment (damn those assertive Black women), and most importantly, raise their status in society. This is not to say that interracial relationships cannot be healthy regardless of why or how they begin. However, prior to getting involved, it's important to recognize the sometimes unconscious motivation behind the choices one makes.

DID YOU KNOW: In 1958 a White man (Richard Loving) married a Black woman (Mildred Jeter) in Virginia and because of it both were criminally indicted. In 1967, after years of legal wrangling, the U.S. Supreme Court finally determined that national anti-miscegenation (anti-interracial marriage) legislation was unconstitutional. And finally in the year 2000, Alabama agreed and removed anti-miscegenation statutes from their state constitution.

47. Why do Black women have a problem with Black male interracial relationships?

The Black woman still hoping to date or marry a Black man may see interracial relationships as a threat to her odds. The slim pickings among marriageable Black men are further thinned by high rates of incarceration, low life expectancy, and homosexuality. As a result, some Black women are frustrated by the recognition that they don't have the luxury of holding out for the best Black prospect. On the other hand, the idea that Black women are so embittered by interracial relationships only benefits Black men and increases their cachet. It's a love war out there and in this case, Black men are the spoils. For those women not holding out for a Black man, there's no problem. Finding compatibility and true love is tough enough without adding racial qualifiers and I think a lot of Black women are waking up to that fact.

TOP 5 Reasons
To Stick With Your Own Kind

5. Seal and Heidi Klum
    (something is just not right there)
4. Janet Jackson and Justin Timberlake
    (prime time Black breast…not okay!)
3. Terrell Owens and Nicolette Sheridan
    (The N.F.L. just courts trouble, doesn't it?)
2. Kobe Bryant and his alleged victim Katelyn Faber
    (I think it's okay to say her name post pay-off)
1. O.J. and Nicole (enough said)

48. Why do Black people prefer menthol cigarettes?

Target marketing.

49. Why can't Black people swim?

It's our diminished lung capacity and dense muscularity that causes us to sink in any body of water. **Just kidding**. Of course some Black people can and do swim. One reason <u>more</u> Black folks don't swim competitively is a lack of access and the prohibitive cost of the sport. Secondly, and more relevant is the reinforcing power of the stereotype. Currently swimming is seen as a "White" sport. If you learn growing up that Black people can't or don't swim, you probably won't swim either. I believe a Black person will eventually dominate the professional field and this tale will finally die.

On another note, you'll notice many Black women going to great lengths to avoid moisture let alone swimming. This is because a few drops of water can cause their chemically straightened hair to "go back" – that is return to its natural texture (not desirable).

V.
TRADITIONS /PROFESSIONAL LIFE
(Same as it Ever Was)

Each of us has at least two personas. The one we project at work and the one our family sees. The workplace is a socially constructed environment where people are not free to be themselves. Work is where social mores are heavily regulated and we're all supposed to be on our best behavior. It's also the place where most standard interaction between Blacks and non-Blacks takes place. Given all the big brother activity, it's difficult to really get to know whom you're dealing with.

As far as developing friendships, the workplace creates the illusion of closeness while you're only actually relating on a superficial level. There's nothing wrong with that in itself. Frequently that's all we want from our co-workers. On the other hand, you shouldn't congratulate yourself on having "lots of Black friends" if your primary experience of them is through work. While visiting someone in his or her home is not the final measure of intimacy, it is guaranteed to give you a far better understanding, if that is what you desire. It's like the way you suddenly *get* your significant other once you see them interact with their family. So if you want to really get to know your black friends, I recommend visiting their church, home or attending a non-work related social event.

Additionally, there are other barriers to getting to know your Black friend at work. Black folks face different sociological challenges (some of it self-imposed) and a pressing level of scrutiny in the workplace. Depending on the environment, Black folks know they immediately stand out by virtue of their skin color. They also know that their errors will tend to be magnified but not necessarily their accomplishments. It can lead to them both you and them wondering, "did I get the job because I'm Black?" Some Black people remedy this by working twice as hard to make up for the fact that you might believe them to be incapable or undeserving. Others simply meet you at your low level of expectation, doing just enough to keep their jobs. It's a heavy psychological load in addition to the day-to-day office politicking, but it's one that many Blacks carry.

You can't imagine how burdensome it is to be constantly judged against a negative standard and know that the majority of people are unwilling (or too scared) to take the time to learn the truth. And you just thought we were being anti-social.

50. Why should I be punished through affirmative action?

Although it feels punitive, affirmative action is intended to redress past wrongs. Presently, Whites reap the benefit of past injustice regardless of whether they're active or passive recipients of favor. And in fact, it is White women who most benefit from affirmative action programs. Many White people are certain that they lost out on a college slot, job, or promotion because it was given to an unqualified Black person. Your anger at Black folks is entirely misdirected; we are not to blame for the current cycle of foolishness. On the other hand, we are always willing to discuss other means of redress (See Question # 6 re: reparations).

In theory, "affirmative action" is a move towards equal treatment, but to its opponents, it is shorthand for quotas, reverse discrimination, and the hiring of unqualified Blacks. The fact is that there are plenty of qualified minorities out there and you probably work alongside some of them. Furthermore, it has been shown that a diverse staff is a boon to an employer's bottom line. No <u>intelligent</u> employer would fill a quota (real or imagined) with an unqualified minority candidate forfeiting productivity and greater profits. Eventually that person would have to be terminated leaving the company vulnerable to a discrimination lawsuit. How dumb is that?

51. Why don't Blacks get along better in the workplace?

Many Blacks have been told and believe that hard work is what gets you ahead. As it turns out that's not entirely true. The formula for success at work is unequal parts who you know, hard work, and garnering favor. Blacks are frequently so focused on doing their job and flying under the radar that they altogether miss the popularity part. At the outset, having less in common with the majority of their co-workers makes it a little more difficult for some Blacks to fit in. So while we all dread the daily grind, simply being Black can raise other barriers to advancement.

Over the course of his career, the Black professional will hear (many times over) the following commonplace directives:

Try harder to smile or laugh to make others more comfortable working with you;

Your aggressiveness, assertiveness, seriousness, etc. is impacting your effectiveness; and

Upon voicing concerns about office actions or behaviors, will be told to lighten up and not be so sensitive.

I guess we're supposed to shoulder the burden of easing interpersonal relations.

52. Why are Blacks always grouping together (e.g. at school, in the workplace, etc.)?

Blacks seek each other out for the same reasons as other people. It's normal to identify with people who look like you and presumably share your cultural experiences as a way of feeling more comfortable. Yet this can be as tricky for Blacks as it is for you. We also make erroneous assumptions based on skin color. The color of our skin does not guarantee a specific cultural experience. But, if nothing else Blacks (American or otherwise), can typically bond over the experience of being perceived as "Black" in America.

I'm sad to say that recently, even generic bonding is something a number of Blacks folks try to avoid. Back in the day, you could always count on a greeting, or at least an acknowledgement from unknown Black folks. Now, particularly when non-Blacks are also present, I notice Black people going out of their way to avoid other Blacks – not even making eye contact. It's as though they believe that by ignoring other Blacks, their Blackness will go undetected. One thought about this behavior toward your fellow Black person – divide and conquer.

53. What is Kwanzaa?

Kwanzaa is a secular week long holiday observance created by Black American Dr. Maulena Karenga (aka Ron Everett) in 1966 and celebrated December 26th through January 1st. Kwanzaa was created to introduce and reinforce seven basic values of African culture that contribute to building and strengthening family, community, and culture among African-American and African people throughout the world African community. These values are called the *Nguzo Saba*, Swahili for the Seven Principles. The Principles are: unity, self-determination, collective work and responsibility, cooperative economics, purpose, creativity and faith. Wow, what a mouthful. I had to research that one myself. Now that you know what it is, odds are you would need to explain it to a Black person. Contrary to what Hallmark has led you to believe, only about 12% of Black people celebrate Kwanzaa. And yes I know Dr. Karenga is a shady character (to say the least), but this question is a question about Kwanzaa.

54. Why is the church so important to the Black community?

The importance of the Black church has its foundation in slavery. Settlers converted Africans brought to the U.S. and as a result Christianity is the principal religion among Black Americans. In the past, church was the place where Blacks could openly communicate and relax away from the watchful eyes of the slave master. Relationships were forged and nurtured and critical information was passed among attendees. In America today, Sunday is said to be the most segregated day of the week. The church is still the place where Black folks can relax in familiar company, enjoy a sense of community, and can let loose without fear of external judgment (in-house judgment is another issue).

55. Why is the preacher so revered in the Black community?

Since you now understand the importance of the church (see Question #54), it stands to reason that the head of the church is the vital part. Church is the place where community business gets done. There is a long history of Black leaders rising from a religious foundation to lead the Black community (Martin Luther King, Jr., Malcolm X, Jesse Jackson), and I expect this trend to continue. Today's politicians know that easy wide-ranging access to community influence comes through the head of the church. That gives that person a lot of power – and responsibility. Unfortunately, some of them are religious charlatans who are unworthy of the trust placed in them.

56. Why do Blacks follow Jesse Jackson and Al Sharpton?

Speaking of charlatans (see Question #55), I don't know any Black folks who follow Jackson or Sharpton. However, just like you, we do follow their antics. Both Reverends have done admirable things in the past, but now they're struggling to stay relevant. It's a shame really because there's so much they could be doing for Black folks. Instead, Jackson and Sharpton are currently competing for national airtime to prove they are the H.N.I.C. (Head Negro in Charge). It's a cold world out there when your primary audience could care less about you – always on the lookout for the next photo opportunity. Here's an idea: pitch yourself as a sitcom or reality television star (Sharpton) or make sure you're the guy to eulogize every celebrated Black person (Jackson).

Moral Leadership Gone Awry
(aka keep it in your pants)

The Honorable Elijah Muhammad
Reverend Martin Luther King, Jr.
Reverend Jesse Jackson
Reverend Al Sharpton
Dr. William Henry "Bill" Cosby

57. Why are Blacks so anti-immigrant?

Americans are generally xenophobic and Black folks are no different. However, I've found the anti-immigrant sentiment to be more prevalent among less educated and lower income Blacks. Upon entering the U.S., many Latino immigrants experience similar socioeconomic circumstances as poor Blacks. They move into economically depressed Black neighborhoods (that were once all White) and find themselves competing with Blacks for crumbs. The adversarial positions created by this dynamic are bad for both groups. With shifting ethnic demographics (i.e. more Latinos) I fully expect these tensions to extend beyond poor Blacks into wider society.

While making a case for Mexican immigration into the U.S., Mexican President Vicente Fox stated that immigrants "take the jobs that not even Blacks want to do." While many wrote off his statement as racist, there is truth to what he said. It has been interesting to watch the change of the employment guard in blue collar, home care, and civil service jobs away from Blacks to Latinos. Many Blacks feel they are slowly being displaced socially, politically, and economically – something that creates feelings of animosity towards immigrants.

Blacks have also experienced problems with some Asian groups in their neighborhoods. Typically these encounters are with merchants who are seen as opportunistic price gougers with no personal stake in the communities where they set up shop.

58. Why are so many Blacks Democrats?

Many Blacks are instinctively faithful to the Democratic Party through a Civil Rights Era connection. It seems unbelievable now, but at one time Republicans were the party of choice for Blacks. It was all about Abraham Lincoln and emancipation. Over time, Blacks have come to see Democrats as the party with their best interests at heart – through social programs, favorable legislative drives, and an expressed identification with certain social values. And ever since Blacks have pledged a blind allegiance to the Democratic Party, they have been taken for granted. Black folks desperately need to critically assess their commitment to the Democrats or any other Party. The photo ops and election year mega church visits are simply not enough.

And while we're on the subject, majority Black interests are not aligned with those Black Republicans trotted out as proof of the Party's commitment to diversity. Blacks should ask of both Parties: what have you done for me lately?

59. Why do so many Blacks become Muslims?

First it should be noted there is a difference between traditional Islam (Muslims) and the Nation of Islam ("NOI" – Black Muslims). For instance, Malcolm X began as a Black Muslim and later became a Muslim.

Some Blacks see Christianity as the White man's religion foisted upon enslaved Africans and recycled down. The fair-haired, blue-eyed Caucasian image of Jesus also turns off many Blacks. Since only a miniscule number of Blacks practice Eastern religions and Jews don't proselytize, Elijah Muhammad and Louis Farrakhan (Black Muslims) were able to fill a spiritual void in Black America with their philosophy of self-reliance based in Afrocentric ideology. As for traditional Islam, I believe Blacks are drawn to messages of equality, brotherhood, social responsibility – and clearly delineated gender roles.

60. Why are Blacks so against homosexuality?

Believe it or not, on a few issues (e.g. gay marriage and abortion) Blacks are fundamentally conservative (hear that Republican Party?). Reared in households deeply rooted in Christianity, Blacks learn early and often that homosexuality is an abomination. As a result, it becomes very important for Black men to appear hyper-masculine and they go to great lengths (extreme homophobia) to maintain that image. There are few things worse to a Black man than a challenge to his masculinity. Clearly they (and much of society) equate manhood with sexual preference. So what becomes of all these denied and repressed behaviors? I'll tell you what: furtive and unsafe sexual activity (the down-low). This current scourge of the Black community has become so prevalent that Oprah devoted an entire show to discussing the problem. Somehow we've all got to get comfortable talking openly about these things (race, sexuality, poverty, etc.).

VI.
CRIMINAL ELEMENT
(It's Not All Good)

I think we can all agree that that the Black male is the boogeyman of American society. Ever notice that the vast majority of those found to have been wrongfully accused and imprisoned is Black? That's because if there is a Black man on or near the scene of a crime (or sometimes just readily available) he'll be charged and likely convicted. In the minds of many, it logically follows that if he was there, then he must be guilty.

Of course, it is a little more complicated than that. I believe it's all about context. For example, Jemahl the Black guy from your accounting department can count on some measure of respect in the office setting. Because you've seen him in that role you accept that it's possible for him to operate in that capacity. However, when you see Jemahl in the parking garage dressed in workout clothes, your internal alarm is set off. Your stereotype based fears about Black males triggers knee jerk avoidance tactics. Remember, only his clothing has changed – and the context. You don't know any more or less about him, but the change in context has prompted a behavioral change. And I'm not saying that you shouldn't use your best judgment and/or common sense, fear can be a very useful tool. However, the odds are that when you enter the office elevator or parking garage with Jemahl (or someone who looks like him) he is not going to mug you. There is no reason to tense up, guard your person or skip the elevator altogether.

Unfortunately these scenarios are fairly commonplace to Jemahl. But you should recognize that the outcome influences not only your future interactions with Jemahl but with all other persons of color (particularly males). In other words, expecting and then manifesting the worst typically causes a negative effect on all future exchanges. The terrible practice of attributing the negative characteristics of one to the whole can be particularly detrimental to Black/White relations. For example, if one white guy beats you up, you hate that guy. But if one Black guy beats you up you hate all Blacks. It's a strange way to operate in the world and yet we all do it to some extent. However, there's no real harm in operating under the assumption that White people can't dance. On the other hand, you're creating a world of unnecessary fear and tension (for yourself and otherwise) if you're going around thinking every Black man is out to get you...the boogeyman indeed.

Worst Trend in Criminal Justice:

BLAME THE BLACK MAN

Each of these individuals wisely blamed
a Black man to throw the police off their trail:

2001 Chris Pittman
(12 years old – killed his grandparents)

1994 Susan Smith (drowned her children)

1992 Jesse Anderson (killed his wife)

1989 Charles Stuart (killed his wife)

61. Why did Blacks side with Rodney King, O.J. Simpson, and Kobe Bryant?

There are different reasons for each case, but they have one thing in common. After years of what Black folks have seen as unfair treatment in the judicial system, the overriding desire is almost always to see a Black man come through unscathed. Nevertheless, you shouldn't take siding with these individuals as Blacks' belief in their innocence.

Rodney King: Blacks were simply dumfounded by the magnitude of injustice in this case. It almost doesn't matter what he did, a videotaped full-scale beating should have been a slam dunk win.

O.J. Simpson: I don't know anyone who felt any ethnic identification with the Juice. Nonetheless, his case was the first real indication to Blacks (and many Whites) that the scales of justice tip in favor of money.

Kobe Bryant: As far as ethnic identification, his case was not too different from O.J.'s case. However, Kobe garnered favor as the symbol of all the Black men whose fate has hung (sometimes literally) on the testimony of a complaining White female.

BLACK WHEN IT'S CONVENIENT

When the chips were down, these people knew they could count on "their people":

O.J. Simpson, Michael Jackson, Kobe Bryant

62. Why are so many Black men in jail?

Since the disparate treatment of Black men in the criminal justice system is well documented, this question is easily answered. Here's the equation: racial profiling that leads to actual criminal activity plus inequitable sentencing equals lots of incarcerated Black men. And lest you think I'm a conspiracy nut, please understand that among other things, this is about money. Housing prisoners is one of the fastest growing industries in the U.S. and it's rapidly being privatized.

63. Why are so many Black men on drugs?

I understand why you would have this idea, but it is actually an incorrect assumption. It appears as though more Black men are on drugs because their use frequently becomes known through racial profiling. Additionally, thanks to racial profiling and the attendant discrimination, drug use by non-Blacks frequently goes undetected and/or is overlooked. However, this is changing now that methamphetamine use is becoming so prevalent, mostly in the White community. The ravages from its use are quite obvious. It will be interesting to see if the majority consumers of meth (non-Blacks) will impact the way the War on Drugs is waged. My guess is that there will be a lot more cries for judicial leniency and rehabilitative measures.

On Being Black – Reality Check

When was the last time YOU:

Held your breath while watching the news, hoping the perpetrator of a crime was not of your race? [Blacks do this because they know that the actions of one will reflect upon them personally.]

Realized you were being followed around a store because you were seen as a security threat?

Knew you could anticipate harassment by law enforcement officials?

64. Why is the pimp culture so elevated in the Black community?

The pimp or drug dealer is often a model of success in the Black community. He has access to subjugated women, drives expensive cars, and appears to have money to spare. Sounds like the set up for all unoriginal hip-hop videos doesn't it? Speaking of videos, you can thank Viacom/MTV and other mainstream media outlets for helping to normalize pimping in general society (*Pimp My Ride, Hustle & Flow, Get Rich or Die Tryin'*). In 2004 Sony Pictures was set to release a cartoon movie about a little White kid that is mentored in and excels at pimping – as an escape from his boring suburban life. Thankfully they were pressured out of widespread release. Who green lights these projects? Not Black people.

And now for the ultimate cultural blessing, the Academy has conferred an Oscar® for Best Original

Song, penned about the difficulty of pimp life. As far as media depictions, it seems like Black people were better off in those few early years before MTV allowed Black artists to air their videos.

65. Why is there so much Black on Black violence?

In blighted and impoverished communities, survival of the fittest is the law of the land. The inhabitants of these neighborhoods have no sense of responsibility for their life condition nor do they have any idea where to direct their frustration and anger. As a result, the nearest (weakest) target bears the brunt of their rage. Black men are aware how little value society places on their lives. Ultimately they see themselves, and those who look like them, in the same worthless light. Some say it's an outward projection of self-loathing with deadly consequences. It's strange; I've yet to encounter a land-owning gangbanger, but they all have a terminal stake in their neighborhood plots of rented space. Fighting and dying over someone else's crumbs and assumed vendettas – makes no sense.

66. Why do Blacks disrespect their women?

In our patriarchal society all women are second-class citizens. It was Yoko Ono who said (and ironically John Lennon gets credited) "woman is the nigger of the world." Imagine then how much more true this is for Black women. Black women are subordinate to Black men who already hold a diminished place in society. As the weaker sex, we are easy targets for disrespect and violence (see Answer #65). However, contrary to what your local music video channel would have you believe, this is not any more true in the Black community than in society in general. On a national level, there is no greater disrespect than the fact that a woman earns less money than a man for equal work – regardless of the color of anybody's skin.

On Being Black – Reality Check

When was the last time YOU:

Thought about how to conceal your race in order to maintain a fair opportunity in any circumstance?

Wondered whether you would receive inferior medical care or prejudicial treatment in the legal system because of the color of your skin?

Wondered if your skin color might prevent you from getting the home loan or apartment of your choice?

Closing

It is often said that a little knowledge can be a dangerous thing. So what are you supposed to do with all this new information? It would help if both Blacks and non-Blacks behaved as though they had no expectation of poor treatment and nothing to fear. Find a happy medium between your life experience and what you've learned here and act accordingly. And most importantly treat people the way you want to be treated. There's nothing more to it than that. Thanks for reading. Peace.

Recommendations

For Blacks:

Give to your non-Black friends as a conversation starter or ender (e.g. you should read this fascinating book or please, don't ask me anymore questions), for book clubs or simply for another perspective.

For non-Blacks:

Good for international readers, interracial daters, recent immigrants and just good for you generally.

Sample letter

Dear _____:

I am giving you this book out of friendship and maybe just a bit of frustration. I hope that reading this book will lead to an open honest discussion so we can really begin to understand one another. Some of the stuff in the book is true but other parts are crap. I would hate for you to read this book and come away with the wrong idea. Let's talk when you're finished reading.

Sincerely,

_____

Your Black friend

ORDER FORM

Why Do Black People Love Fried Chicken? And Other Questions You've Wondered But Didn't Dare Ask

Online: Order direct from: www.yourblackfriend.com

By mail: Your Black Friend
                P.O. Box 1532
                Venice, CA 90294

E-mail: author@yourblackfriend.com

Please print

Name: _____

Address:_____

City: _____ State: _____ Zip:_____

E-mail: _____

Quantity _____@ $10.00

Please add $3.95 Shipping and Handling
California residents please add $1.00 (7.25%) sales tax

Index

Work...3, 17, 19, 24, 38, 46, 49, 51, 61-63, 65, 77